C0-BKV-915

Thoughts for My Daughters

Eloise Lovelace

authorHOUSE®

AuthorHouse™
1663 Liberty Drive
Bloomington, IN 47403
www.authorhouse.com
Phone: 1-800-839-8640

© 2011 Eloise Lovelace. All rights reserved.

No part of this book may be reproduced, stored in a retrieval system, or transmitted by any means without the written permission of the author.

First published by AuthorHouse   11/16/2011

ISBN: 978-1-4670-6640-2 (sc)
ISBN: 978-1-4670-6637-2 (e)

Printed in the United States of America

Any people depicted in stock imagery provided by Thinkstock are models, and such images are being used for illustrative purposes only.
Certain stock imagery © Thinkstock.

This book is printed on acid-free paper.

Because of the dynamic nature of the Internet, any web addresses or links contained in this book may have changed since publication and may no longer be valid. The views expressed in this work are solely those of the author and do not necessarily reflect the views of the publisher, and the publisher hereby disclaims any responsibility for them.

Dedication

For my daughters Kristina and Theresa who have created rich and rewarding lives for themselves and their families, and for my husband Norm who has been a loving father to these two beautiful young women.

Preface

Some of these thoughts are truths I have learned over the past sixty years. Others are beliefs or opinions I have formulated from a lifetime of positive social interactions and rewarding experiences and learning. They by no means exhaust the list of topics but are instead thoughts that have mattered to me. It is my hope that whoever reads this book may benefit or be inspired by these insights, even if only to become aware of a new perspective.

On Attitudes

Live with a positive attitude, with the belief that things will work out. By being positive, you tend to work harder to achieve your goal, you enjoy the journey more, you have a greater appreciation of the outcome, and you build on your own feelings of self worth.

On Babies

Even with a colicky, fussy or naughty baby, appreciate every moment. Babies change so fast that if you don't take in every moment, you'll wonder where the time went (you'll wonder it anyway). A young child's personality is made up of so many different facets, he or she needs them all to develop into a well rounded individual.

On Birds

Birds signify the freedom, beauty and tenuousness of nature. In flight we see the freedom, and in the beckoning call of the bird we see the beauty of untamed nature. We are also reminded of the power and responsibility of man over the creatures of the world.

On Birth

The birth of a child is a miracle that cannot be duplicated. No matter the sex, color, characters, features or abilities, each is a unique individual that warrants the unbiased love of his parents.

On Books

Books provide an escape into another world. They inform, humor, create emotions, and simply pass time. There is nothing quite like the pictures that come to life in conjunction with the story, the turning of pages or the smell of an old book. They are treasured keepsakes of times past and foretellers of our futures.

On Change

Change is often difficult to look forward to,
but reaps benefits for those involved. Even the
most difficult of changes may bring families or
friends closer together, and breaks us out of a
mold we find ourselves in. It puts us in a more
flexible state of mind.

On Children

Children learn what they see. In order to instill in the child a high standard of self-worth, a parent must create a positive environment, give the child guidance, be open to new ideas, dare to be spontaneous, search for new experiences for the child, realize that defiance is a way of exerting one's opinion, allow the child to make decisions, ask the child's opinion, and above all, be openly lovable with the child.

On College

Although college is a tool in the attainment of one's goals or the achievement of knowledge, its most beneficial aspect is the openness it bestows in one's mind in regards to varying attitudes and beliefs.

On Contemplation

Take time to be alone and contemplate your life. Looking inward at your beliefs brings peace to the soul.

On Daughters

Daughters are precious. A daughter can be your best friend, one with whom you share your secrets and one who cares for you no matter what. Through daughters and your grandchildren, your legacy lives on.

On Disabilities

Disabilities are only one small part of a person's being. No matter the disability, each of us is born with many beautiful aspects to the personality. A person with a disability will outshine others in many ways.

On Dogs

Dogs give unconditional love. They greet you, follow you around, give comfort when you are sad, are easy to forgive, and provide friendship that does not depend on similar attitudes. All they ask for, in return, is a healthy lifestyle, fun in the form of exercise, obedience training and loving from you. Every family, who is physically able, should provide their children with the experience of owning a dog.

On the Elderly

Grant them the respect they've earned. They have lived long lives, have gained much knowledge, some of which you will never learn, and have contributed much to their families and friends. They have their bodies and sometimes their minds slowly walking out on them, and have the end of their lives to look forward to. They deserve the love and attention you can give them, if only to lend an ear.

On Empathy

Empathy is a wonderful attribute to possess. By confirming a child's or teenager's thoughts or feelings, you show you're thinking of them. Empathy shows others how much you care, and makes yourself a more giving and sensitive person. If in doubt whether or not to empathize with a person, ask yourself how you would feel in the same situation.

On Equality

All of man is created equal. We should never make judgements or harbor biased thoughts based on color, sex or sexual preferences, religion or cultural differences. With true equality, the world would be a peaceful place in which to live.

On Friends

True friends accept each other's personalities,
yet share common bonds that bring them
together. The strength of a friendship is
measured in part by the ability to compromise
or to come back together after a minor storm.

On Hunting

Man should never kill animals for sport. Other beings have as much right to live on this earth as does man. Man is only one creature in the perpetuation of life, and his life is better for having shared this earth with other creatures.

On Love

Love is the warmth in your heart when you think of a person. Love is wanting the best for that person, even if that best differs from your own desires. Love is wanting a peaceful solution after you are angry. Love is the excitement you feel as you come together after being apart. Love is all-encompassing.

On Marriage

Marriage is a union of two people who love each other, rather than a melding of two personalities into one. Embrace yourself as an individual, for only when you can accept and love your own personality can you truly embrace the other's. Look forward to both the time alone and to the sharing with your spouse.

On Modesty

Show humility in your acceptance of praise. People would much prefer associating with someone who is unpretentious or down to earth than someone who is arrogant.

On Music

Creating or listening to beautiful music brings
peace and contentment to the soul.

On Nature

Always appreciate the natural beauty surrounding you. Take time to listen to the rain on the roof, the birds overhead, the wind rustling the trees, the water cascading down the hill or the crickets chirping at night. The towering trees, exotic wildflowers, majestic mountains, oceans and rivers are what give this earth a beauty not to be taken lightly. All of the creatures, whether they are the magnificent lion, the stately giraffe, the scavenging seagull or the lowly banana slug remind us of our place on this earth.

On Observation

Take time to look at the world through the eyes of a child. Notice the caterpillar, watch how the leaf blows, see the shape in the cloud. You will slow yourself down, marvel along with the child and find enjoyment in, and appreciation for, the little things.

On the Ocean

The ocean is all powerful, letting nothing stand in its way. It puts our lives in perspective, makes us humble, shows us that natures does and should have its way. Try to find a way to fall asleep at night listening to the waves. It will make you appreciate its power and put you at peace.

On Parents and Grandparents

Remember that these people raised you, and you turned out okay. Give them the respect they deserve. If their parenting opinions are different than your own, listen to their ideas. Afterward, if your opinions are still different, gently explain yours, then as a parent you are entitled to make the final decision. Although an older person may have a more difficult time raising or tending to a child, he or she misses that closeness that being a parent brings. Involve them in your life as much as possible.

On Rain

Rain is precious and refreshing. It shows nature and science at work, and refreshes the earth around us. What better way to lull you to sleep than the patter of raindrops on the roof. Unless it destroys life around us, there can never be too much rain.

On Rainbows

Rainbows are a beautiful sight to behold, one that cannot be duplicated. They are a spark in one's life, brightening one's day.

On Siblings

All children should have the experience of growing up with at least one brother or sister. A sibling provides a child with a confidant and playmate, teaches a child to share, provides an environment that makes spoiling difficult, and becomes a friend for life in a way that no one else can.

On Smiles

Give smiles freely. They brighten your face, portray the idea that you are interested in others, and brighten others' days. They are contagious and make the world a better place. Nothing lights up one's eyes as being told they have a beautiful smile.

On Spontaneity

Do not be afraid to be spontaneous in your actions. By saying yes to a reasonable request of your child's or spouse's, you not only please them but you also portray yourself as a fun-loving and giving person.

On Stress

Try to put a rein on your emotional stress. Stress acts in a negative way on your mind and your body. No matter the circumstances, there is always someone worse off than you. By relaxing and remaining in a calm state of mind, you increase your enjoyment in life and set a positive example for others.

On Teenagers

Teenagers have a rough road to follow. Their hormones are changing, their brains are not fully developed, they are forced into being independent in school, they must start making decisions about the future. At the same time they're looked upon to stop playing the childhood games they have always engaged in. Involve them in any decision making, ask their opinions, willingly allow them time alone or with friends. Remember, as a parent, you are learning also.

On Trains

Hearing the rumble, clickety-clack and drawn-out whistle of a steam train creates wonderful feelings of nostalgia. Take your children on a train ride so they too can experience the freedom and openness of riding the rails.

On Travel

Travel while you can. You never know what life brings. Acquaint yourself with other ways of life as much as possible. You will develop a more rounded personality, enriching the person you are, and be more tolerant of other ways of life.

On War

War is, and always will be, a debatable subject
as to its causes. An individual or nation must
fight for its independence and yet nations not
directly involved should restrain from joining in
and bringing about the loss of innocent lives.

On the Wind

Wind, as it blows through or around whatever stands in its way, symbolizes freedom, the freedom to think and feel how we desire. Whatever the obstacle, we can stand behind our beliefs.

On Life

Live your life to the fullest. Appreciate all the beautiful moments. Use the unpleasant times to learn from. Give of yourself as much as you can. Show your love with a complement, a generous deed or a gift from the heart. Remember, in the end, it won't matter how much money or what type of job you have. These are only a means to the end. You will be remembered for the love you give your family and for the caring you give to friends and strangers alike.